T0193179

La ley del embudo
The Law of the Funnel
A Bilingual Story

Written by Ana Monnar
Illustrated by Anna Lee Monnar

Order this book online at www.trafford.com
or email orders@trafford.com

Most Trafford titles are also available at major online book retailers.

Trafford www.trafford.com
PUBLISHING®
North America & international
toll-free: 844-688-6899 (USA & Canada)
fax: 812 355 4082

Readers Are Leaders U.S.A., Inc.
www.ReadersAreLeadersUSA.net

Our mission is to efficiently provide the world's finest, most comprehensive book publishing service, enabling every author to experience success. To find out how to publish your book, your way, and have it available worldwide, visit us online at www.trafford.com

ISBN: 978-1-4120-1287-4 (sc)

Print information available on the last page.

Trafford rev. 02/19/2021

Este libro está dedicado para todas las personas del mundo que no son egoistas.

This book is dedicated to all the unselfish people of the world.

En este mundo de dar y recibir, algunas personas no tienen un buen balance.

In this world of give and take, some people don't have a good balance.

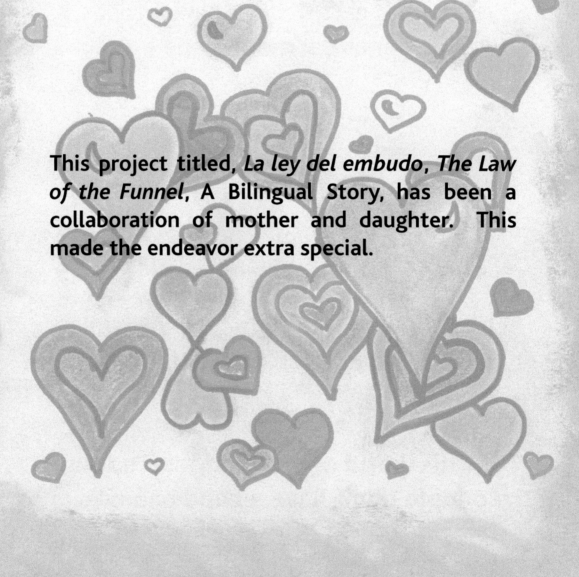

This project titled, *La ley del embudo*, *The Law of the Funnel*, A Bilingual Story, has been a collaboration of mother and daughter. This made the endeavor extra special.

¿Alguna vez ha usted conocido a una persona, qué dice durante su mayor parte del tiempo, "Yo, yo y yo?"

Have you ever met a person
who mostly says, "Me, me, me?"

Esa persona piensa que el mundo gira alrededor de ella.

That person thinks the world revolves around them.

Ya es tiempo para que abra los ojos y pueda ver que la vida no es así.

It's time to open her eyes to see.

Usted quizás se sacrifique y le haga muchos favores, acerca de 100 favores quizás séan.

You might go out of your way to do favors, about 100 favors it might be.

Pero en el favor número 101, puede ser que usted no
pueda hacerlo,
y bien brava esa persona se pondrá.

But on the 101st you just can't do it and upset
that person will be.

Esa persona cree que la parte ancha del embudo siempre
es para ella.

That person believes that the wide part of the
funnel is always meant for them.

Entonces la parte delgada del embudo, el resto del
mundo puede obtener.

Then the thin part of the funnel, the rest of
the world can get.

¡De repente un despertar no muy agradable! Finalmente la confirmación de que la vida no funciona de esa manera.

All of a sudden a rude awakening! Finally the realization that it just doesn't work that way.

Es mucho mejor dar que recibir.

It's better to give sparingly, than to be on
the receiving end.

Las personas que son desinteresadas, están mas contentos de sí mismo.

People who are unselfish are happier with themselves.

Durante su vida, ellos han
estado dando, del corazón le viene, naturalmente.

During their lifetime they have been giving,
from the heart it comes naturally.

Cuando ellos necesitan sinceramente ayuda, Dios les mandará ángeles en su camino. Entonces sea agradecido, humilde y recuerde decir, "Gracias Dios por los Angeles que usted me mandó cada día."

When they truly need help, God will send Angels their way.
Then be grateful, appreciative and humble, plus remember
what to say, "Thank you God for the Angels that you sent
each and everyday."

About the Author

Ana Monnar is married to Octavio Monnar. They both were blessed with three children, Alberto, Anna and Alexander. The family also adopted Lulu, the star Yorkshire Terrier. Sunny, a Yellow Nape parrot has been with the family for many years.

Mrs. Monnar has been teaching for 25 years. She is currently teaching fourth grade. Other books written by Ana Monnar are titled, *Half Full, Or Half Empty? A Collection of Poems, Poetry from Planet Earth, Adoption? Thank God for That Option!* (English and Spanish versions), *The Law of the Funnel* (English and Spanish/English bilingual versions) and *It Doesn't Matter!*

About the Illustrator

Anna Monnar is the daughter of Ana and Octavio Monnar. She has two brothers, Alberto and Alexander. She is also blessed with her older sister, Alina. Her sister Alina is from Mr. Monnar's first marriage.

Anna took many years of dance lessons. From age four to age 11, she danced ballet, lyrical, tap and jazz. Anna is currently 12 years old. She reads the second reading during mass every month. She loves and participates in track and field, cross country, basketball, softball, volleyball, and enjoys being in team sports at school. Anna is very much loved by her family and friends. The teachers and the administrators at the Catholic School where Anna attends show a lot of love and care also.

Printed in the United States
By Bookmasters